The Joyful Mysteries

The Joyful Mysteries
Copyright © 2023
Sara Swann

ISBN: 978-1-957344-84-3

Cover design by Mike Parker
Illustrations copyright © 2023 by Sara Swann. Used by permission, all rights reserved.

Published by WordCrafts Press
Cody, Wyoming 82414
www.wordcrafts.net

The Joyful Mysteries

Mysteries of the Rosary for Children
Volume 1

SARA SWANN

WordCrafts Press

To my beautiful Michaela. You have been my greatest joy since the day I learned I was destined to be your mother, and you continue to be a blessing not only to me, but to everyone you meet. You make Mama so proud. I thank God for you daily, and I love you to the moon and back.

GETTING STARTED

The first step in praying your Rosary is to get ready. For each mystery below, the prayers you pray will be written in **bold**, so you know what to say, just like the responses you say in Mass, and their Latin translations are there in ***bold italics***, too.

Now, look at your Rosary. Every Rosary has a crucifix, a medallion, six big beads, and 53 smaller beads. All these beads help us pray lots of prayers, and that is just one of the many reasons that make the Rosary so special.

You might be asking, what prayers go where? There are only seven prayers you need to know to pray the Rosary.

1. The Sign of the Cross
2. The Apostles' Creed
3. The Hail Mary
4. The Glory Be
5. The Fatima Prayer
6. The Hail Holy Queen
7. The Final Prayer.

The Sign of the Cross always bookends, or begins and ends, the Rosary just as it begins and ends all our prayers.

The Crucifix is for the Apostle's Creed. The big beads are

for the Our Father prayer, and the small beads are for the Hail Mary. The other prayers are sprinkled throughout.

Are you ready to get started?

Let's go!

MONDAY AND SATURDAY
(And Sundays during the Advent season)

The Joyful Mysteries

During these Joyful Mysteries, you will walk with Mary and Joseph as they learn that God chose them to be the parents of His Son, Jesus Christ.

> **Did you know . . .**
> We pray these mysteries on Mondays, Saturdays, and during the Advent and Christmas season Sundays, too.

Begin with your Rosary in your hand.

Do the Sign of the Cross by touching your Rosary to your forehead, then your chest, then left shoulder, then your right shoulder.

> **Did you know . . .**
> There is a very important difference between a cross and a Crucifix? A Crucifix is a cross with Jesus's body, called The Corpus, on it!

You can remember this because God the Father is in Heaven above us (touch your forehead), God the Son lives in your heart (touch your chest), and Jesus carried the Cross on His shoulders (touch your left shoulder then your right shoulder). When you say amen, put your hands together in front of you, like prayer hands.

In the name of the Father,

In nomine Patris,

(Forehead)

and of the Son,

et Filii,

(Chest or Heart)

and of the Holy Spirit.

Et Spiritus Sancti.

(Left then Right Shoulder)

Amen.

Amen.

(End with prayer hands)

Now you are ready to begin praying your Rosary. First, hold the Crucifix and pray the Apostles' Creed.

I believe in God,

Credo in Deum

the Father almighty,

Patrem omnipoténtem,

Creator of heaven and earth,

Creatórem cæli et terræ.

And in Jesus Christ,

Et in Iesum Christum,

His only Son,

Fílium eius únicum,

Our Lord,

Dóminum nostrum,

Who was conceived by the Holy Spirit,

qui concéptus est de Spíritu Sancto,

Born of the Virgin Mary,

natus ex María Vírgine,

Suffered under Pontius Pilate,

passus sub Póntio Piláto,

Was crucified, died, and was buried;

crucifíxus, mórtuus, et sepúltus,

He descended into hell;

descéndit ad ínfernos,

On the third day;

tértia die;

He rose again from the dead;

resurréxit a mórtuis;

He ascended into Heaven,

ascéndit ad cælos,

And is seated at the right hand of God,

sedet ad déxteram Dei,

The Father Almighty,

Patris omnipoténtis,

And from there He will come

inde ventúrus

to judge the living and the dead.

est iudicáre vivos et mórtuos.

I believe in the Holy Spirit,

Credo in Spíritum Sanctum,

The Holy Catholic Church,

sanctam Ecclésiam cathólicam,

The communion of Saints,

sanctórum communiónem,

The forgiveness of sins,

remissiónem peccatórum,

The resurrection of the body,

carnis resurrectiónem,

And life everlasting.

vitam ætérnam.

Amen.

Amen.

Now, move your fingers up to the next bead. It is bigger than the other beads and may even be a different color, so you know this bead is for the Our Father prayer.

Our Father, who art in heaven,

Pater noster, qui es in cælis,

hallowed be Thy name.

sanctificétur nomen tuum.

Thy kingdom come,

Advéniat regnum tuum.

Thy will be done,

Fiat volúntas tua,

On earth as it is in heaven.

sicut in cælo, et in terra.

And give us this day our daily bread,

Panem nostrum quotidiánum da nobis hódie,

And forgive us our trespasses,

et dimítte nobis débita nostra sicut

As we forgive those who trespass against us,

et nos dimíttimus debitóribus nostris.

And lead us not into temptation,

Et ne nos indúcas in tentatiónem,

But deliver us from evil.

sed líbera nos a malo.

Amen.

6

Amen.

Next, we have three small beads. You already know these are for the Hail Mary prayers. Each one of these three beads are special for a different reason. These special beads help open our hearts to be more like Mother Mary in our own *Faith*, *Hope*, and *Charity*.

Did you know . . .
Charity is love.

Move your fingers to the first Hail Mary bead. This Hail Mary bead is the *Faith* bead. We ask for an increase in our Faith as we pray the Hail Mary prayer.

Hail Mary, full of grace,
> *Ave María, grátia plena,*

the Lord is with thee.
> *Dóminus tecum.*

Blessed art thou amongst women,
> *Benedícta tu in muliéribus,*

and blessed is the fruit of thy womb, Jesus.
> *et benedíctus fructus ventris tui, Iesus.*

Holy Mary, Mother of God,
> *Sancta María, Mater Dei,*

Pray for us sinners,
> *ora pro nobis peccatóribus,*

Now and at the hour of our death.
> *nunc, et in hora mortis nostræ.*

Amen.
> *Amen.*

Now, move your fingers to the second small bead. On this bead, we pray the Hail Mary prayer and ask for an increase in our *Hope*.

Hail Mary, full of grace,

Ave María, grátia plena,

the Lord is with thee.

Dóminus tecum.

Blessed art thou amongst women,

Benedícta tu in muliéribus,

and blessed is the fruit of thy womb, Jesus.

et benedíctus fructus ventris tui,Iesus.

Holy Mary, Mother of God,

Sancta María, Mater Dei,

Pray for us sinners,

ora pro nobis peccatóribus,

Now and at the hour of our death.

nunc, et in hora mortis nostræ.

Amen.

Amen.

Finally, move your fingers to the third small bead. On this bead, we pray the Hail Mary prayer and ask for an increase in our *Charity*.

Hail Mary, full of grace,

Ave María, grátia plena,

the Lord is with thee.

Dóminus tecum.

Blessed art thou amongst women,

Benedícta tu in muliéribus,

and blessed is the fruit of thy womb, Jesus.

et benedíctus fructus ventris tui, Iesus.

Holy Mary, Mother of God,

Sancta María, Mater Dei,

Pray for us sinners,

ora pro nobis peccatóribus,

Now and at the hour of our death.

nunc, et in hora mortis nostræ.

Amen.

Amen.

Remember those surprise prayers we talked about earlier? Here is the first time you find them in the Rosary!

With your fingers still on the bead, you say two very special prayers. First, is the Glory Be.

When you say the Glory Be prayer, you bow to the Crucifix to show respect and love to Jesus Christ.

Then, you say the Fatima Prayer. Sometimes, the Fatima Prayer is sometimes called the O My Jesus prayer.

> **Did you remember . . .**
> to bow to your crucifix whenever
> you pray a Glory Be?

Glory Be

Glória

to the Father,

Patri,

and to the Son,

et Fílio,

and to the Holy Spirit.

et Spirítui Sancto.

As it was in the beginning,

Sicut erat in princípio,

Is now,

et nunc,

And ever shall be,

et semper,

World without end.

et in sæcula sæculórum.

Amen.

Amen.

Then, pray your Fatima Prayer.

O My Jesus,

Dómine Jesu,

Forgive us our sins,

dimitte nobis débita nostra,

And save us from the fires of hell.

salva nos ab igne inferni,

Lead all souls to heaven,

perduc in caelum omnes ánimas,

Especially those in most need of thy

praesertim eas, quae misericórdiae tuae

mercy.

máxime indigent.

Now you're ready to begin your first Joyful Mystery!

The First Joyful Mystery

The Annunciation of Our Lord

The First Joyful Mystery comes from the Gospel of St. Luke. The Scripture for the first Joyful Mystery tells us why this mystery is important.

In the sixth month the angel Gabriel was sent from God to a city of Galilee named Nazareth, to a virgin betrothed to a man whose name was Joseph, of the house of David; and the virgin's name was Mary. And he came to her and said, "Hail, full of grace, the Lord is with you!" But she was greatly troubled at the saying and considered in her mind what sort of greeting this might be. And the angel said to her, "Do not be afraid, Mary, for you have found favor with God. And behold, you will conceive in your womb and bear a son, and you shall call his name Jesus.

He will be great and will be called the Son of the Most High; and the Lord God will give to him the throne of his father David, and he will reign over the house of Jacob forever; and of his kingdom there will be no end."

And Mary said to the angel, "How shall this be, since I have no husband?"

And the angel said to her, "The Holy Spirit will come upon you,

and the power of the Most High will overshadow you; therefore the child to be born will be called holy, the Son of God.

And behold, your kinswoman Elizabeth in her old age has also conceived a son; and this is the sixth month with her who was called barren. For with God nothing will be impossible."

And Mary said, "Behold, I am the handmaid of the Lord; let it be to me according to your word."

And the angel departed from her.

St. Luke 1:26–38.

Move up to the next big bead. Remember, this is an Our Father bead.

Our Father, who art in heaven,

Pater noster, qui es in cælis,

hallowed be Thy name.

sanctificétur nomen tuum.

Thy kingdom come,

Advéniat regnum tuum.

Thy will be done,

Fiat volúntas tua,

On earth as it is in heaven.

sicut in cælo, et in terra.

And give us this day our daily bread,

Panem nostrum quotidiánum da nobis hódie,

And forgive us our trespasses,

et dimítte nobis débita nostra sicut

As we forgive those who trespass against us,

et nos dimíttimus debitóribus nostris.

And lead us not into temptation,

Et ne nos indúcas in tentatiónem,

But deliver us from evil.

sed líbera nos a malo.

Amen.

Amen.

```
┌─────────────────────────────────────┐
│ Thoughts to Consider. . .           │
│  As we pray this mystery, we think  │
│ about how we can be more modest     │
│ and humble each day. Modesty and    │
│ humility are the fruits of this     │
│ mystery.                            │
└─────────────────────────────────────┘
```

Next, pray ten Hail Mary prayers while you think about the Scripture. We also think about how we can be more modest and humble.

Hail Mary, full of grace,

Ave María, grátia plena,

the Lord is with thee.

Dóminus tecum.

Blessed art thou amongst women,

Benedícta tu in muliéribus,

and blessed is the fruit of thy womb, Jesus.

et benedíctus fructus ventris tui, Iesus.

Holy Mary, Mother of God,

Sancta María, Mater Dei,

Pray for us sinners,

ora pro nobis peccatóribus,

Now and at the hour of our death.

nunc, et in hora mortis nostræ.

Amen.

Amen.

Pro Tip . . .

Move to the next bead each time you say amen.

Remember the two special prayers, The Glory Be and The Fatima Prayer, that are hidden throughout our Rosary? You just found them again! Keep holding the tenth bead and pray a Glory Be and a Fatima Prayer. Remember to bow to your Crucifix when you pray your Glory Be.

Glory Be

Glória

to the Father,

Patri,

and to the Son,

et Fílio,

and to the Holy Spirit.

et Spirítui Sancto.

As it was in the beginning,

Sicut erat in princípio,

Is now,

et nunc,

And ever shall be,

et semper,

World without end.

et in sæcula sæculórum.

Amen.

Amen.

Did you know . . .
Another word for annunciation is announcement.

Then, pray your Fatima Prayer.

O My Jesus,

Dómine Jesu,

Forgive us our sins,

dimitte nobis débita nostra,

And save us from the fires of hell.

salva nos ab igne inferni,

Lead all souls to heaven,

perduc in caelum omnes ánimas,

Especially those in most need of thy

praesertim eas, quae misericórdiae tuae

mercy.

máxime indigent.

Congratulations! You have just finished praying your first decade of the Rosary! As you prayed, you thought about how you can be humble and modest in your own life, just like Mary and Joseph. Think of some ways you can be modest and humble in your life. Write down some of your thoughts on the next page.

Did you know . . .
The Rosary is divided into sets of ten Hail Mary prayers called decades. There are five decades in one full Rosary.

The Second Joyful Mystery

The Visitation of Our Lord

The Second Joyful Mystery comes from the Gospel of St. Luke and tells us why this mystery is important.

In those days Mary arose and went with haste into the hill country, to a city of Judah, and she entered the house of Zechariah and greeted Elizabeth. And when Elizabeth heard the greeting of Mary, the babe leaped in her womb; and Elizabeth was filled with the Holy Spirit and she exclaimed with a loud cry, "Blessed are you among women, and blessed is the fruit of your womb! And why is this granted me, that the mother of my Lord should come to me? For behold, when the voice of your greeting came to my ears, the babe in my womb leaped for joy. And blessed is she who believed that there would be a fulfillment of what was spoken to her from the Lord."
St. Luke 1:39–45

Thoughts to Consider . . .

The fruit of this mystery is to love your neighbor. How can you show Jesus's love to your friends, relatives, and neighbors?

Move your fingers to the next big, Our Father bead.

Our Father, who art in heaven,
> *Pater noster, qui es in cælis,*

hallowed be Thy name.
> *sanctificétur nomen tuum.*

Thy kingdom come,
> *Advéniat regnum tuum.*

Thy will be done,
> *Fiat volúntas tua,*

On earth as it is in heaven.
> *sicut in cælo, et in terra.*

And give us this day our daily bread,

Panem nostrum quotidiánum da nobis hódie,

And forgive us our trespasses,

et dimítte nobis débita nostra sicut

As we forgive those who trespass against us,

et nos dimíttimus debitóribus nostris.

And lead us not into temptation,

Et ne nos indúcas in tentatiónem,

But deliver us from evil.

sed líbera nos a malo.

Amen.

Amen.

Move your fingers along the beads as you pray ten Hail Mary prayers and think about the Scripture. Also think about ways you can show Jesus's love to others.

Hail Mary, full of grace,

Ave María, grátia plena,

the Lord is with thee.

Dóminus tecum.

Blessed art thou amongst women,

Benedícta tu in muliéribus,

and blessed is the fruit of thy womb, Jesus.

et benedíctus fructus ventris tui, Iesus.

Holy Mary, Mother of God,

Sancta María, Mater Dei,

Pray for us sinners,

ora pro nobis peccatóribus,

Now and at the hour of our death.

nunc, et in hora mortis nostræ.

Amen.

Amen.

> **Did you know . . .**
> All the mysteries of the Rosary are taken from Scripture.

Keep holding the tenth bead and pray a Glory Be and a Fatima Prayer. Remember to bow to your crucifix when you pray your Glory Be.

Glory Be

Glória

to the Father,

Patri,

and to the Son,

et Fílio,

and to the Holy Spirit.

et Spirítui Sancto.

As it was in the beginning,

Sicut erat in princípio,

Is now,

et nunc,

And ever shall be,

et semper,

World without end.

et in sæcula sæculórum.

Amen.

Amen.

Then, pray your Fatima Prayer.

O My Jesus,

Dómine Jesu,

Forgive us our sins,

dimitte nobis débita nostra,

And save us from the fires of hell.

salva nos ab igne inferni,

Lead all souls to heaven,

perduc in caelum omnes ánimas,

Especially those in most need of thy

praesertim eas, quae misericórdiae tuae

mercy.

máxime indigent.

> **Did you know . . .**
> The first person who recognized the Christ child in Scripture was an unborn child.

How about that! You have just finished praying your second decade of the Rosary!

As you prayed, you thought about how you can show Jesus's love to others. Write down some of your ideas how to do this on the next page.

The Third Joyful Mystery

The Nativity of Our Lord

The Third Joyful Mystery comes from the Gospel of St. Luke.

Did you know . . .
This mystery tells us the Christmas story.

In those days a decree went out from Caesar Augustus that all the world should be enrolled. This was the first enrollment, when Quirinius was governor of Syria. And all went to be enrolled, each to his own city. And Joseph also went up from Galilee, from the city of Nazareth, to Judea, to the city of David, which is called Bethlehem, because he was of the house and lineage of David, to be enrolled with Mary, his betrothed, who was with child. And while they were there, the time came for her to be delivered. And she gave birth to her first-born son and wrapped him in swaddling clothes, and laid him in a manger, because there was no place for them in the inn.

And in that region there were shepherds out in the field, keeping watch over their flock by night. And an angel of the Lord appeared to them, and the glory of the Lord shone around them, and they were filled with fear. And the angel said to them, "Be not afraid; for behold, I bring you good news of a great joy which will come to all the people; for to you is born this day in the city of David a Savior, who is Christ the Lord. And this will be a sign for you: you will find a babe wrapped in swaddling clothes and lying in a manger." And suddenly there was with the angel a multitude of the heavenly host praising God and saying,

"Glory to God in the highest, and on earth peace among men with whom he is pleased!"

St. Luke 2:1-14

Thoughts to Consider . . .
The fruit of this mystery is poverty. How can you show your detachment from worldly goods like The Holy Family did the night Jesus was born?

Move your fingers to the next big, Our Father bead.

Our Father, who art in heaven,
Pater noster, qui es in cælis,
hallowed be Thy name.
sanctificétur nomen tuum.
Thy kingdom come,
Advéniat regnum tuum.
Thy will be done,
Fiat volúntas tua,
On earth as it is in heaven.
sicut in cælo, et in terra.
And give us this day our daily bread,
Panem nostrum quotidiánum da nobis hódie,
And forgive us our trespasses,
dimítte nobis débita nostra sicut
As we forgive those who trespass against us,
et nos dimíttimus debitóribus nostris.
And lead us not into temptation,
Et ne nos indúcas in tentatiónem,
But deliver us from evil.
sed líbera nos a malo.
Amen.
Amen.

Move your fingers along the beads as you pray ten Hail Mary prayers and think about the Scripture. Also think about ways you can show Jesus's love to others.

Hail Mary, full of grace,

Ave María, grátia plena,

the Lord is with thee.

Dóminus tecum.

Blessed art thou amongst women,

Benedícta tu in muliéribus,

and blessed is the fruit of thy womb, Jesus.

et benedíctus fructus ventris tui, Iesus.

Holy Mary, Mother of God,

Sancta María, Mater Dei,

Pray for us sinners,

ora pro nobis peccatóribus,

Now and at the hour of our death.

nunc, et in hora mortis nostræ.

Amen.

Amen.

Keep holding the tenth bead and pray a Glory Be and a Fatima Prayer. Remember to bow to your crucifix when you pray your Glory Be.

Glory Be

Glória

to the Father,

Patri,

and to the Son,

et Fílio,

and to the Holy Spirit.

et Spirítui Sancto.

As it was in the beginning,

Sicut erat in princípio,

Is now,

et nunc,

And ever shall be,

et semper,

World without end.

et in sæcula sæculórum.

Amen.

Amen.

> **Did you know . . .**
> The Fatima Prayer came from Mother Mary herself when she appeared to three poor, shepherd children in Fatima, Portugal in 1917.

Now, it's time for the Fatima Prayer.

O My Jesus,

Dómine Jesu,

Forgive us our sins,

dimitte nobis débita nostra,

And save us from the fires of hell.

salva nos ab igne inferni.

Lead all souls to heaven,

perduc in caelum omnes ánimas,

Especially those in most need of thy

praesertim eas, quae misericórdiae tuae

mercy.

máxime indigent.

Great job! You have just finished praying your third decade of the Rosary!

As you prayed, you thought about how Mary and Joseph were not given any room in the inn but were made to take shelter in a stable with the animals to bring baby Jesus into the world. What are some ways you can be like the The Holy Family on the night Jesus was born? Write down some of your ideas how to be like The Holy Family on the next page.

The Fourth Joyful Mystery

The Presentation of Our Lord at the Temple

T he Fourth Joyful Mystery comes from the Gospel of St. Luke

*And when the time came for their purification accord-
ing to the law of Moses, they brought him up to Jerusalem
to present him to the Lord (as it is written in the law of
the Lord, "Every male that opens the womb shall be called
holy to the Lord") and to offer a sacrifice according to what
is said in the law of the Lord, "a pair of turtledoves, or
two young pigeons." Now there was a man in Jerusalem,
whose name was Simeon, and this man was righteous
and devout, looking for the consolation of Israel, and the
Holy Spirit was upon him. And it had been revealed to
him by the Holy Spirit that he should not see death before
he had seen the Lord's Christ. And inspired by the Spirit
he came into the temple; and when the parents brought
in the child Jesus, to do for him according to the custom
of the law, he took him up in his arms and blessed God
and said,*

> *"Lord, now lettest thou thy servant depart in peace,*
> *according to thy word;*
> *for mine eyes have seen thy salvation*
> *which thou hast prepared in the presence of all peoples,*
> *a light for revelation to the Gentiles,*
> *and for glory to thy people Israel."*

*And his father and his mother marveled at what was
said about him; and Simeon blessed them and said to
Mary his mother,*

> *"Behold, this child is set for the fall and rising of many
> in Israel, and for a sign that is spoken against (and a
> sword will pierce through your own soul also), that
> thoughts out of many hearts may be revealed."*

*And there was a prophetess, Anna, the daughter of
Phanu-el, of the tribe of Asher; she was of a great age,
having lived with her husband seven years from her
virginity, and as a widow till she was eighty-four. She*

did not depart from the temple, worshiping with fasting and prayer night and day. And coming up at that very hour she gave thanks to God and spoke of him to all who were looking for the redemption of Jerusalem.

St. Luke 2:22–38

Thoughts to Consider . . .
The fruit of this mystery is obedience.

Move your fingers to the next big, Our Father bead.

Our Father, who art in heaven,

> *Pater noster, qui es in cælis,*

hallowed be Thy name.

> *sanctificétur nomen tuum.*

Thy kingdom come,

> *Advéniat regnum tuum.*

Thy will be done,

> *Fiat volúntas tua,*

On earth as it is in heaven.

> *sicut in cælo, et in terra.*

And give us this day our daily bread,

> *Panem nostrum quotidiánum da nobis hódie,*

And forgive us our trespasses,

> *et dimítte nobis débita nostra sicut*

As we forgive those who trespass against us,

> *et nos dimíttimus debitóribus nostris.*

And lead us not into temptation,

> *Et ne nos indúcas in tentatiónem,*

But deliver us from evil.

> *sed líbera nos a malo.*

Amen.

Amen.

Move your fingers along the beads as you pray ten Hail Mary prayers and think about the Scripture. Also think about ways you can show obedience in your life.

Hail Mary, full of grace,

Ave María, grátia plena,

the Lord is with thee.

Dóminus tecum.

Blessed art thou amongst women,

Benedícta tu in muliéribus,

and blessed is the fruit of thy womb, Jesus.

et benedíctus fructus ventris tui, Iesus.

Holy Mary, Mother of God,

Sancta María, Mater Dei,

Pray for us sinners,

ora pro nobis peccatóribus,

Now and at the hour of our death.

nunc, et in hora mortis nostræ.

Amen.

Amen.

Keep holding the tenth bead and pray a Glory Be and a Fatima Prayer. Remember to bow to your crucifix when you pray your Glory Be.

Did you know . . .
The Glory Be is also known as the doxology, or by its Latin name, Gloria Patri.

Glory Be

Glória

to the Father,

Patri,

and to the Son,

et Fílio,

and to the Holy Spirit.

et Spirítui Sancto.

As it was in the beginning,

Sicut erat in princípio,

Is now,

et nunc,

And ever shall be,

et semper,

World without end.

et in sæcula sæculórum.

Amen.

Amen.

Now, it's time for the Fatima Prayer.

O My Jesus,

Dómine Jesu,

Forgive us our sins,

dimitte nobis débita nostra,

And save us from the fires of hell.

salva nos ab igne inferni,

Lead all souls to heaven,

perduc in caelum omnes ánimas,

Especially those in most need of thy

praesertim eas, quae misericórdiae tuae

mercy.

máxime indigent.

Look how far you've come! You have just finished praying your fourth decade of the Rosary!

As you prayed, you thought about how Mary and Joseph were obedient to the ways of their Jewish customs. What are some ways you can be obedient like the The Holy Family when they presented baby Jesus to Simeon at the temple. Write down some of your ideas about how to be like The Holy Family on the next page.

_____

_____

_____

_____

_____

_____

_____

_____

_____

_____

_____

_____

_____

_____

_____

_____

_____

_____

_____

_____

_____

_____

_____

_____

_____

_____

_____

_____

_____

_____

_____

_____

_____

The Fifth Joyful Mystery

Finding Jesus in the Temple

The Fifth Joyful Mystery comes from the Gospel of St. Luke.

Now his parents went to Jerusalem every year at the feast of the Passover. And when he was twelve years old, they went up according to custom; and when the feast was ended, as they were returning, the boy Jesus stayed behind in Jerusalem. His parents did not know it, but supposing him to be in the company they went a day's journey, and they sought him among their kinsfolk and acquaintances; and when they did not find him, they returned to Jerusalem, seeking him. After three days they found him in the temple, sitting among the teachers, listening to them and asking them questions; and all who heard him were amazed at his understanding and his answers. And when they saw him they were astonished; and his mother said to him, "Son, why have you treated us so? Behold, your father and I have been looking for you anxiously." And he said to them, "How is it that you sought me? Did you not know that I must be in my Father's house?" And they did not understand the saying which he spoke to them. And he went down with them and came to Nazareth, and was obedient to them; and his mother kept all these things in her heart.

And Jesus increased in wisdom and in stature, and in favor with God and man.

St. Luke 2:41–52

Thoughts to Consider . . .
The fruit of this mystery is devotion to Jesus.

Move your fingers to the next big, Our Father bead.

Our Father, who art in heaven,

Pater noster, qui es in cælis,

hallowed be Thy name.

sanctificétur nomen tuum.

Thy kingdom come,

Advéniat regnum tuum.

Thy will be done,

Fiat volúntas tua,

On earth as it is in heaven.

sicut in cælo, et in terra.

And give us this day our daily bread,

Panem nostrum quotidiánum da nobis hódie,

And forgive us our trespasses,

et dimítte nobis débita nostra sicut

As we forgive those who trespass against us,

et nos dimíttimus debitóribus nostris.

And lead us not into temptation,

Et ne nos indúcas in tentatiónem,

But deliver us from evil.

sed líbera nos a malo.

Amen.

Amen.

Move your fingers along the beads as you pray ten Hail Mary prayers and think about the Scripture. Think about how The Holy Family must have felt when they could not find twelve-year-old Jesus for three days, then found him in the temple!

Hail Mary, full of grace,

Ave María, grátia plena,

the Lord is with thee.

Dóminus tecum.

Blessed art thou amongst women,

Benedícta tu in muliéribus,

and blessed is the fruit of thy womb, Jesus.

et benedíctus fructus ventris tui, Iesus.

Holy Mary, Mother of God,

Sancta María, Mater Dei,

Pray for us sinners,

ora pro nobis peccatóribus,

Now and at the hour of our death.

nunc, et in hora mortis nostræ.

Amen.

Amen.

Keep holding the tenth bead and pray a Glory Be and a Fatima Prayer. Remember to bow to your crucifix when you pray your Glory Be.

Glory Be

Glória

to the Father,

Patri,

and to the Son,

et Fílio,

and to the Holy Spirit.

et Spirítui Sancto.

As it was in the beginning,

Sicut erat in princípio,

Is now,

et nunc,

And ever shall be,

et semper,

World without end.

et in sæcula sæculórum.

Amen.

Amen.

Now, it's time for the Fatima Prayer.

O My Jesus,

Dómine Jesu,

Forgive us our sins,

dimitte nobis débita nostra,

And save us from the fires of hell.

salva nos ab igne inferni,

Lead all souls to heaven,

perduc in caelum omnes ánimas,

Especially those in most need of thy

praesertim eas, quae misericórdiae tuae

mercy.

máxime indigent.

You're almost finished praying your first entire mystery of the Rosary!

Did you know . . .

Every mystery of this Joyful Mystery came from the Gospel of St. Luke.

As you prayed, you thought about how Mary and Joseph felt as they searched for young Jesus. How must it have felt to find the child Jesus in the Temple after three days of searching for Him? Write down some of your ideas about how they must have felt when they found Jesus in the Temple on the next page.

_____
_____
_____
_____
_____
_____
_____
_____
_____
_____
_____
_____
_____
_____
_____
_____
_____
_____
_____
_____
_____
_____
_____
_____
_____
_____
_____
_____
_____

The Mystery of the Rosary

The Ending of Each Mystery

The ending of each Mystery of the Rosary consists of two very special prayers: The Hail Holy Queen and The Final Prayer.

Hail Holy Queen

Hail Holy Queen,

Salve Regína,

Mother of Mercy,

mater misericórdiæ;

our Life, our Sweetness, and our hope.

vita, dulcédo, et spes nostra, salve.

To thee we cry,

Ad te Clamámus

poor banished children of Eve.

éxsules fílii Evæ;

To thee we send up our sighs,

Ad te Suspirámus,

mourning and weeping in this valley of tears.

geméntes et flentes in hac lacrimárum valle.

Turn then most gracious advocate,

Eia ergo, Advocáta nostra,

Thine eyes of mercy toward us,

Illos tuos misericórdes óculos ad nos convérte:

and after this, our exile,

Et Iesum, benedíctum fructum

show unto us,

ventris tui, Nobis post hoc exsílium

the blessed fruit of thy womb, Jesus.

osténde.

O clement, O loving, O sweet Virgin Mary.

O clemens, o pia, o dulcis Virgo María.

Pray for us O Holy Mother of God,

Ora pro nobis, Sancta Dei Genetrix.

that we may be made worthy

Ut digni efficiamur

of the promises of Christ.

promissiónibus Christi.

Amen.

Amen.

The Final Prayer ends each Mystery of the Rosary.

Let us pray.

Oremus.

O God, whose only begotten Son,

Déus, cújus Unigénitus

by His life, death, and resurrection,

per vítam, mortem, et resurrectiónem

has purchased for us the

Súam nóbis salútis

rewards of eternal life,

ætérnæ præmia comparávit:

grant, we beseech Thee,

concéde, quæsumus:

that meditating upon these mysteries

ut hæc mystéria

of the Most Holy Rosary of

sacratíssimo beátæ

the Blessed Virgin Mary,

Maríæ Vírginis Rosário recoléntes,

we may imitate what they contain

et imitémur quod cóntinent,

and obtain what they promise,

et quod promíttunt, assequámur.

through the same Christ Our Lord.

Per eúndem Chrístum Dóminum nóstrum.

Amen.

Amen.

Remember what bookends all your prayers—including your Rosary prayers—The Sign of the Cross.

In the name of the Father,

In nomine Patris,

(Forehead)

and of the Son,

et Filii,

(Chest or Heart)

and of the Holy Spirit.

Et Spiritus Sancti.

(Left then Right Shoulder)

Amen.

Amen.

(End with prayer hands)

Acknowledgements

There are so many I would like to thank for helping the Mysteries of the Rosary for Children series come to fruition. My children, who not only stood by me as I taught myself to draw and then to paint in order to create the illustrations for this series, but drew and painted right along with me. My parents, who not only encouraged this project from the beginning, but were just as excited as me as each painting progressed and came to *life*. To my publishers, Mike and Paula, as they championed this project from the beginning, deep within the throes of the pandemic.

> *And the angel said to them: Fear not; for, behold, I bring you good tidings of great joy that shall be to all the people. For today, a Savior has been born for you in the city of David: he is Christ the Lord. And this will be a sign for you: you will find the infant wrapped in swaddling clothes and lying in a manger. And suddenly there was with the Angel a multitude of the celestial army, praising God and saying, Glory to God in the highest, and on earth peace to men of good will.*
>
> *St. Luke 2:10-14 NIV*

Sara Swann-Barnard BSN, RN

ABOUT THE AUTHOR

Sara Swann loves to write and has more than thirty credited works available in print.

She holds a Bachelor of Arts degree in History and spent several years as a teacher in West Texas before earning a Bachelor of Science degree in Nursing. She now works as an emergency room nurse in Houston, Texas, where she, her children, and their menagerie of rescue pets—six in all—make their home.

In her spare time, Sara and her family enjoy ice cream and the beach, but she wishes someone who majored in Physics and Engineering would hurry up and invent a time machine so she could meet St. Francis of Assisi, Henry VIII, William Wallace, and Vlad the Impaler.

Connect with Sara online at:

www.NurseSaraBooks.com

www.ingramcontent.com/pod-product-compliance
Lightning Source LLC
Chambersburg PA
CBHW070944120626
46546CB00004B/1564